MAP SMART

Community Maps

NICOLAS BRASCH

A+

This edition first published in 2012 in the United States of America by Smart Apple Media.

Smart Apple Media
P.O. Box 3263
Mankato, MN, 56002

First published in 2011 by
MACMILLAN EDUCATION AUSTRALIA PTY LTD
15–19 Claremont St, South Yarra, Australia 3141

Visit our web site at www.macmillan.com.au or go directly to www.macmillanlibrary.com.au

Associated companies and representatives throughout the world.

Library of Congress Cataloging-in-Publication Data has been applied for.

Publisher: Carmel Heron
Commissioning Editor: Niki Horin
Managing Editor: Vanessa Lanaway
Editor: Laura Jeanne Gobal
Proofreader: Georgina Garner

Designer: Colby Heppell (text and cover)
Page Layout: Romy Pearse
Photo Researcher: Jes Senbergs (management: Debbie Gallagher)
Illustrator: Ian Faulkner (www.ianfaulknerillustrator.com)
Production Controller: Vanessa Johnson

Manufactured in China by Macmillan Production (Asia) Ltd.
Kwun Tong, Kowloon, Hong Kong
Supplier Code: CP December 2010

Acknowledgments
The author and the publisher are grateful to the following for permission to reproduce copyright material:

Front cover photograph: Aerial view of a residential area in a typical suburban home community in Ontario, Canada, courtesy of 123RF/ Helen Filatova.

Photographs courtesy of: Corbis, **4** (left), /C. Devan, **5**; Federal Agency for Cartography and Geodesy, Frankfurt am Main, Germany, **12**; Getty Images/Altrendo Images, **4** (middle); iStockPhoto/Freeze Frame Studio, **14**, /Lukasz Laska, **8**, /Martti Salmela, **20**; Photolibrary/Westend61, **4** (right); Shutterstock/Willie Cole, **21** (middle left), /Dragana Gerasimoski, **21** (bottom middle right), /Tom Live, **21** (middle top left), /Pedro Talens Masip, **21** (middle right), /S26, **21** (middle bottom left), / Sjgh, **21** (bottom left), **21** (middle top right), /John T Takai, **21** (middle centre left), /VBT, **21** (bottom right), /Z-art, **21** (top right), /Andre Zje, **21** (middle centre right).

Please note
At the time of printing, the Internet addresses appearing in this book were correct. Owing to the dynamic nature of the Internet, however, we cannot guarantee that all these addresses will remain correct.

Contents

When a word is printed in **bold**, you can look up its meaning in the Glossary on page 31.

Be "Map Smart"

Are you "map smart?" Knowing about maps and how to read them is very important. There will be many times in our lives when we will need to use a map. Being "map smart" is a useful skill for life.

What Is a Map?

A map is a drawing of something that gives a person a view of it from above. A map can show the shape and location of countries, small areas of land, natural features, such as rivers, and artificial features, such as roads. There are many types of maps for many different uses.

A map can guide people from one place to another. It can show them where different places are and how far away one place is from another. Maps can save people time and energy by helping them not get lost.

Maps are available in many different forms and people use them in different ways.

Hi! My name is Mapolean, but you can call me Map. I'll pop up from time to time to give you some tips on being "map smart."

Community Maps

Community maps cover an area in which a particular community lives or gathers. The largest community maps cover a single town or city. Smaller community maps are created for parks, shopping malls, schools, and other locations.

What Do Community Maps Show?

Community maps show people all the features within a local area. These features might include:

- walking trails in a park
- a supermarket within a shopping mall
- train stations along a train **route**
- the cafeteria in a school

TRY THIS

The next time you are at a mall, try to find a store you have never been to without looking at a map. Next, try to find a store you have never been to after looking at a map. Which method got you to the store faster?

When Do People Use Community Maps?

People use community maps to find a street they have never been to or to find a store in a shopping mall. A community map can also show people where to catch a train, which train route to travel on, and how many stops there are before they reach their destination.

People can use a community map to find out where to get off a bus.

Types of Community Maps

There are many types of community maps. Different types of community maps show different types of information.

Street Maps

Street maps display all the roads and streets in a certain area.

A street map helps people find their way around a small area of land.

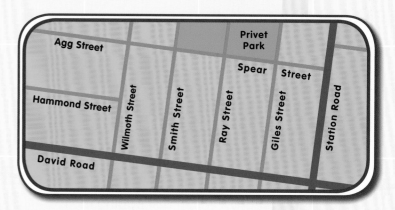

Public Transportation Maps

Public transportation maps show the routes taken by trains, buses, streetcars, ferries, and other types of public transportation. These maps highlight each stop along the route and show how some routes join up with other routes.

The London Underground

The map of the London Underground train system is so famous that it is used as a design on T-shirts, postcards, and tea towels! You can view the map here: http://www.tfl.gov.uk/assets /downloads/standard-tube-map.pdf

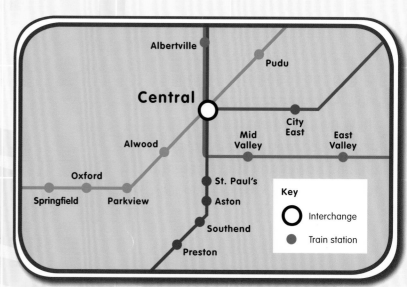

This map shows how different train routes might be linked.

Land Maps

Land maps highlight areas of land where there are no or few buildings, such as parks and walking trails.

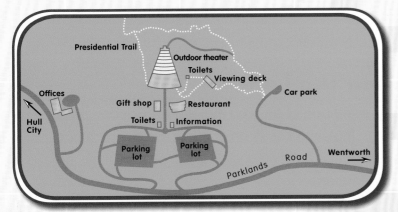

This map of a park shows buildings, roads, and walking trails.

Building Maps

Building maps show all of the rooms and corridors in a building, such as a school or hospital.

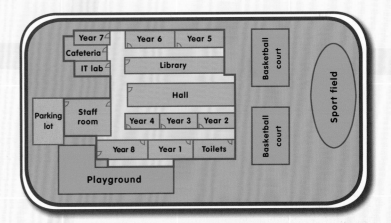

This map helps students to find their way around a school.

Precinct Maps

Precinct maps show a group of buildings within a specific area. A college map, for example, is a precinct map because it shows visitors where all the buildings are on a college **campus**.

Buildings on precinct maps are often marked with a number or letter. A **key** on the side of the map explains which buildings the numbers or letters represent.

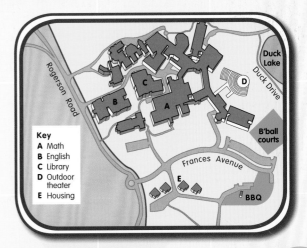

How Is a Community Map Created?

There are six main stages involved in creating a community map. The stages that involve drawing the map are done by a cartographer.

Stage 1: Surveying the Land

Surveying involves inspecting every part of an area that will be included on a map. This can be carried out on foot, in a car, in an airplane, or even in a boat. Surveying also involves measuring the position and **angle** of each feature, as well as the distance between features.

A surveyor uses a device known as a theodolite to measure angles.

Did you know that a person who creates maps is called a cartographer (*car-tog-ra-fa*)? The word "cartographer" comes from the French word *carte*, meaning "map."

Surveying from Space!

Sometimes, surveying is done by **satellites** that take photos of Earth from space. Even though the satellites are very far away, they can take a photo of just one house or a single street.

Stage 2: Deciding What to Include on the Map

Cartographers cannot include every detail on a map. They have to decide which features are important and which ones can be left out. A cartographer mapping a street will not show every twist and turn or every tree and utility pole.

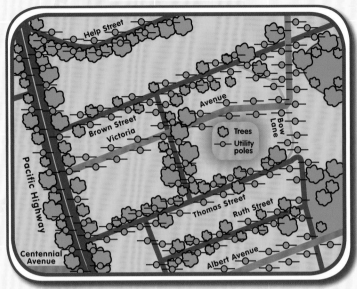

A street map that included every tree and utility pole would be too cluttered and not easy to read.

Stage 3: Deciding On the Scale of the Map

The **scale** of a map is the relationship between the size of the features on the map and their sizes in **reality**. The features cannot be drawn to their actual sizes, so the cartographer has to shrink them. Every feature must be shrunk by exactly the same amount to make the map as **accurate** as possible.

The scale is usually represented on the map in figures. If the scale on a park map is 1:1,000, it means the park on the map is 1,000 times smaller than the park in reality.

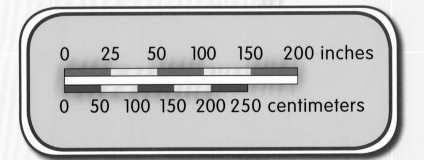

Sometimes the scale appears in the form of a bar that shows what distance each centimeter or inch on the map represents. This scale shows that 1 centimeter is equal to 50 centimeters.

Stage 4: Choosing Symbols for the Map

Symbols are pictures or patterns on a map that represent particular features. Cartographers have to decide what these symbols should be.

Symbols have to be easy to understand and are usually linked to the feature they represent. For example, hospitals might be represented by a red cross, rivers might be represented by the color blue, and sport fields might be represented by a green oval or rectangle. Once readers know what the symbols represent, they can take a quick look at a map and understand where and what everything is.

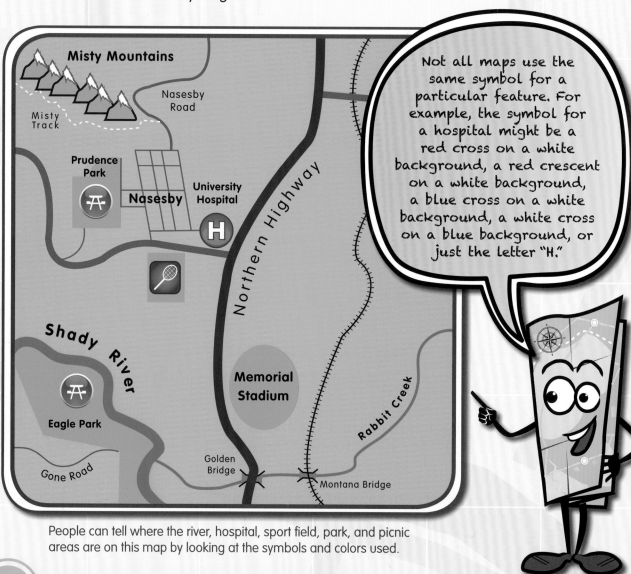

Not all maps use the same symbol for a particular feature. For example, the symbol for a hospital might be a red cross on a white background, a red crescent on a white background, a blue cross on a white background, a white cross on a blue background, or just the letter "H."

People can tell where the river, hospital, sport field, park, and picnic areas are on this map by looking at the symbols and colors used.

Stage 5: Checking the Accuracy of the Map

Once the map is ready, it is checked to make sure it is accurate. For a street map, this may involve driving along every street to check that the routes match what is shown on the map. For a building map, this may involve walking around the building and making sure the rooms are where they appear on the map. Any error must be corrected.

TRY THIS

Check if your local library has an old map of your community. Compare this old map with a more recent version. What differences can you find?

Stage 6: Updating the Map

Keeping maps up-to-date is very important. Some types of community maps are updated and reprinted regularly. When a new street is built, it has to be included in the next version of a street map. Online maps can be updated more quickly and easily than printed versions.

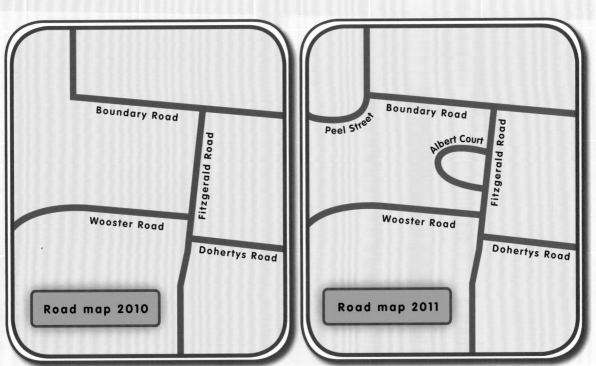

Albert Court and Peel Street have been included in the latest version of this street map.

Features of Community Maps

Community maps have many features that help people read and understand them. Cartographers decide which features they need for the type of map they are creating.

Using Shortcuts

Cartographers use simple designs to represent different map features. Once people know what the designs represent, they can look at a map and immediately understand it. They can think of map features as shortcuts. The main features of most community maps are:

- a compass rose
- a grid
- landmarks
- a scale
- **elevation**
- different colors

A cartographer uses some basic features to represent complicated information on a map.

There is one other feature that a map needs to identify it—a title! Without a title, people wouldn't know which area the map represents.

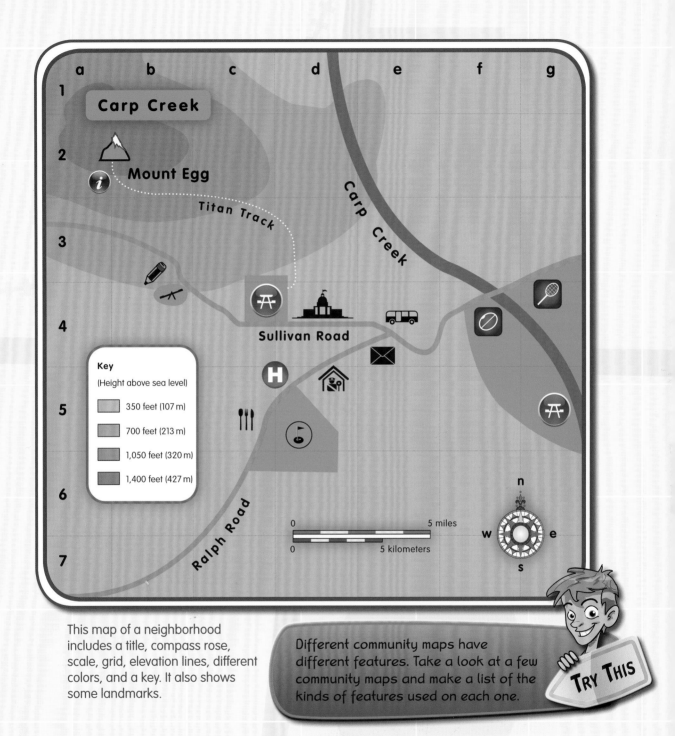

This map of a neighborhood includes a title, compass rose, scale, grid, elevation lines, different colors, and a key. It also shows some landmarks.

Different community maps have different features. Take a look at a few community maps and make a list of the kinds of features used on each one.

TRY THIS

Compass Rose

A compass rose is a feature on a map that indicates direction, such as north, south, west, and east. It shows readers the direction they have to follow to get from one place to another. A compass rose may be placed in a corner of a community map.

The directions on a compass rose are based on those found on a compass. A compass is a device that tells people which way is north, no matter where they are.

There are usually eight points on a compass: N (north), S (south), W (west), E (east), NW (northwest), NE (northeast), SW (southwest), and SE (southeast).

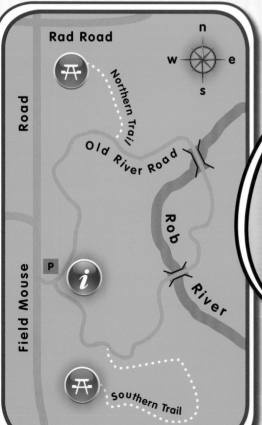

Compass roses can be very simple, showing just a cross with the compass points labeled, or they can be more decorative, such as the one on this map.

Look at the map on this page. Using the compass rose, we can see that to get from the southern picnic ground to the river, we should walk northeast. Using a compass, we can easily tell which way northeast lies.

Pointing North

No matter which direction a compass faces, the needle on the compass always points north. Traveling with a compass and a map with a compass rose will help people reach their destination!

Grid

A grid is a pattern of **horizontal** and **vertical** lines that forms a series of squares, columns, and rows. Each column is given a letter, starting from "A." Each row is given a number, starting from "1."

Locations on a map are often given a grid reference. For example, if a train station is in section F6 on a map, the reader should find the square where column F and row 6 meet. The train station will be within that square.

TRY THIS

Using the map on this page, name the features at A3, G6, and B8.

Answers:
A3—playground;
G6—soccer field;
B8—parking lot.

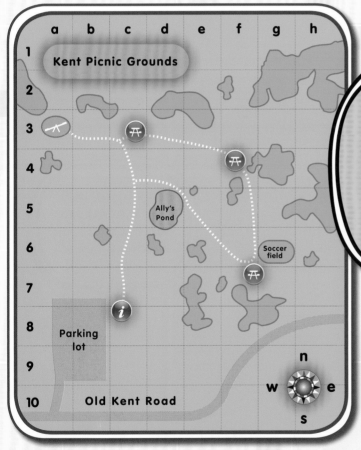

On this map, there is a pond in section D5. To find the pond on the map, move one finger down column D and another finger along row 5. The point where your fingers meet forms section D5. The pond is in this section.

A grid reference makes it easy to find something on a map.

Landmarks

Landmarks are major buildings, objects, and natural features that are easily recognized. When people ask for directions, we usually guide them to their destination by pointing out landmarks they should look out for.

Maps contain the major landmarks people might look for on a map. There are often many landmarks on a map, so symbols are used to represent them.

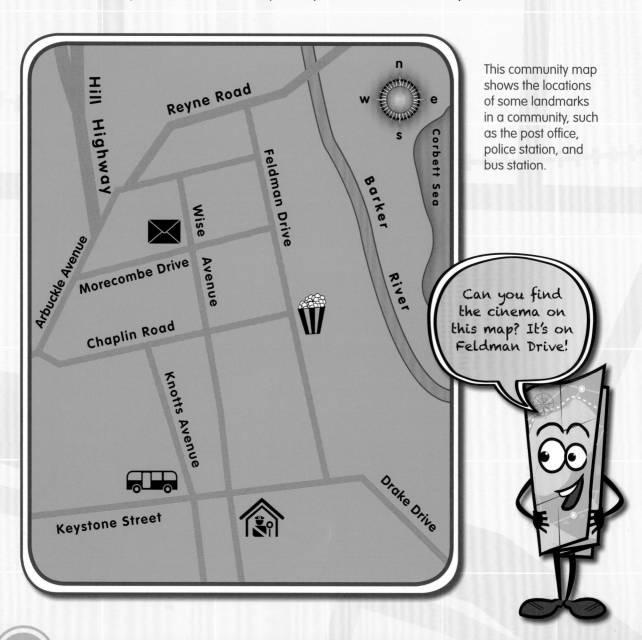

This community map shows the locations of some landmarks in a community, such as the post office, police station, and bus station.

Scale

The scale of a map tells people how much smaller the map is than the area it represents. It is important that everything on a map is reduced by the same amount. If two streets were reduced by different amounts, one street may look longer than the other one on a map even though it may be shorter in **reality**. Reducing everything by the same amount also ensures that the distances between the features on a map are correct.

The scale of a map is usually represented by a bar scale that shows how much each inch or centimeter on a map represents in reality.

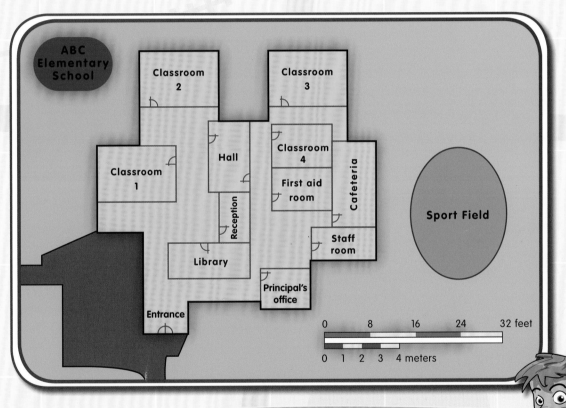

On this map of a school, the scale shows that 1 centimeter on the map is equal to 7 feet (2 m) in reality.

Using a ruler and the scale of the map, figure out the real distance from the door of classroom 2 to the door of the library.

Answer: 26 feet (8 m)

Try This

Elevation

Although a map is flat, the area that it represents is usually not flat. There may be hills, mountains, lakes, or other natural features represented on it. To show these features on a map, cartographers need to show their elevation. Elevation is expressed as feet or meters above sea level. For example, if an area of land has an elevation of 1,000 feet, it is 1,000 feet (305 m) above sea level. Elevation is shown using two methods—different shades of colors and **contour lines**.

Colors are used to show changes in elevation on this map. The key provides information about the elevation represented by each color.

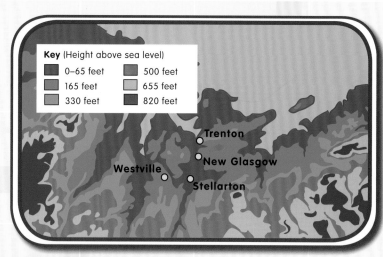

Key (Height above sea level)

- 0–65 feet
- 165 feet
- 330 feet
- 500 feet
- 655 feet
- 820 feet

Trenton
New Glasgow
Westville
Stellarton

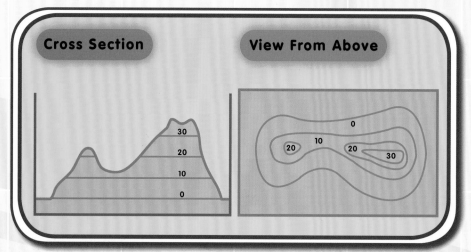

Cross Section

30
20
10
0

View From Above

0
10
20
20
30

The diagram on the left shows the changing elevation of an area of land. The map on the right shows how this is represented with contour lines instead. The numbers refer to how many feet above sea level the area is.

Using Elevation

Elevation is a useful feature on community maps that show bicycle paths, running tracks, and hills. This feature tells athletes wanting to train and people who exercise what to expect before they start their route.

Colors

Colors are used on maps to help identify different features quickly and easily. For example, on a street map, major roads may be colored black, while smaller streets may be gray. The use of different colors helps drivers to find the roads they need easily and tells them what kind of road to expect.

Blue is often used to represent rivers, lakes, and other bodies of water. A quick glance at a map will show readers where all of the bodies of water are.

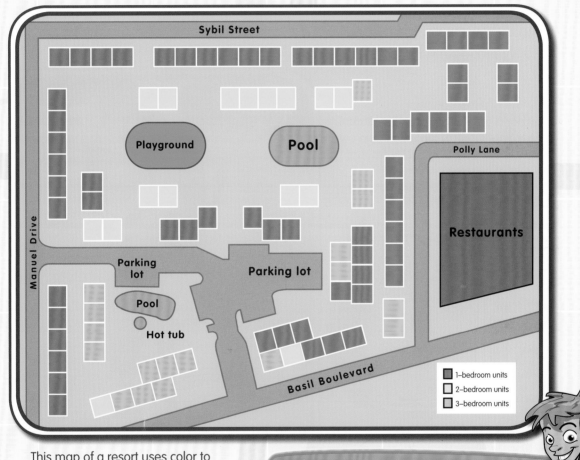

This map of a resort uses color to show the size of the holiday units.

Go to http://maps.google.com and type in your address. What colors are used to represent highways, major roads, streets, parks, rivers, and other features near your home?

Try This

Symbols on Community Maps

Symbols are pictures or patterns that represent particular features. They are used to help readers understand a map.

Quick and Easy

Symbols save cartographers time. For example, by using just a small rectangle to represent a building, a cartographer does not have to spend time surveying the building to draw it **accurately** on the map. Symbols need to be simple and easily recognized by readers.

Symbols are not just found on maps. There are symbols around people every day, such as on footpaths that can also be used by cyclists. How many symbols can you spot on your way to and from school?

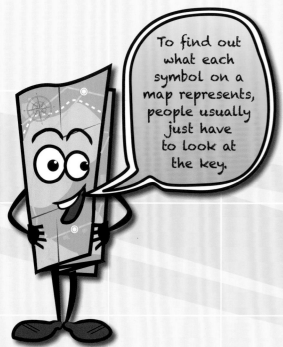

To find out what each symbol on a map represents, people usually just have to look at the key.

Guess the Symbols

Here are some symbols that people might find on a community map. Can you guess what they represent? There is a clue with each one.

(a) A strong swimmer could swim across this.

(b) Stand by for a bumpy landing!

(c) You probably visit this place several times a day.

(d) "A full tank, please!"

(e) This is where you go if you're really sick.

(f) Using this takes less effort than walking.

(g) "Going up!"

(h) If you're on two wheels, stay in this lane.

(i) These **facilities** are not for everyone to use.

(j) "Ouch! I need a bandage!"

(k) Parents need this room for their young children.

(l) "Can I help you?"

Check your answers!
(a) a river *(b)* an airport *(c)* a restroom *(d)* a gas station *(e)* a hospital *(f)* an escalator *(g)* an elevator
(h) a bicycle path *(i)* a restroom for the handicapped *(j)* first aid facilities *(k)* baby changing station
(l) an information desk

Reading Community Maps

Now that you have learned about the different parts of a map, it is time to try reading different types of community maps.

Reading a Street Map

Street maps help people in cars and other vehicles to find their way around unfamiliar streets. Street maps may have a number of common features:

- The compass rose indicates which way north, south, west, and east lie.

- The thick, yellow lines are major roads.

- The white lines are minor roads.

- The curving black line is a train route. The dots along the train route represent railway stations.

- The green areas are parks.

- Picnic areas within parks are symbolized by picnic tables.

- The open books are symbols for schools.

How would you direct people from Orient Grove in section A4 to Gregory Court in section D3, using the map on page 23? Which roads would they travel along and in which directions would they turn?

Go to http://www.openstreetmap.org and use the search and zoom functions to locate the streets in your neighborhood. Print the map and walk around your neighborhood to see if any streets are missing from the map. If there are missing streets, get an adult (such as a parent or teacher) to log on to the site and help them correct the map by adding the missing streets.

TRY THIS

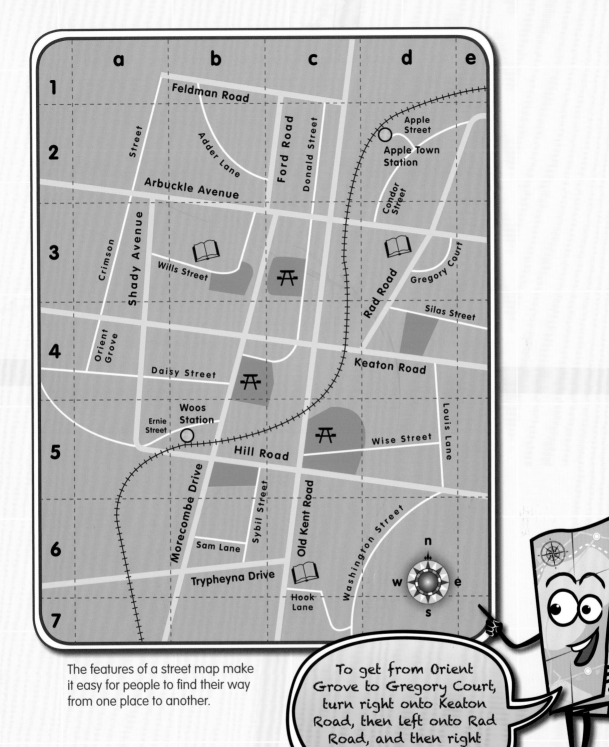

The features of a street map make it easy for people to find their way from one place to another.

To get from Orient Grove to Gregory Court, turn right onto Keaton Road, then left onto Rad Road, and then right onto Gregory Court.

Reading a Public Transportation Map

Public transportation maps help people understand train, bus, streetcar, or ferry routes. Different public transportation maps may have a number of common features:

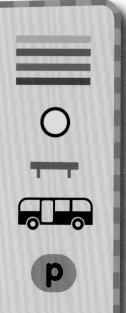

- The green, red, and purple lines indicate train routes.

- The small yellow circles represent major train stations.

- The short lines represent smaller train stations.

- The outline of a bus represents a connecting bus service from the station.

- The letter "p" indicates that there is a parking lot at the station.

How would you direct people traveling from Libra Lane, on the red line, to Soho, on the purple line, using the map on page 25? At which stations would they have to change trains?

Hong Kong's MTR

Hong Kong has one of the busiest public transportation systems in the world. The MTR, or Mass Transit Railway, moves 3.7 million passengers a day! About 90 percent of all travel in Hong Kong is done by public transportation.

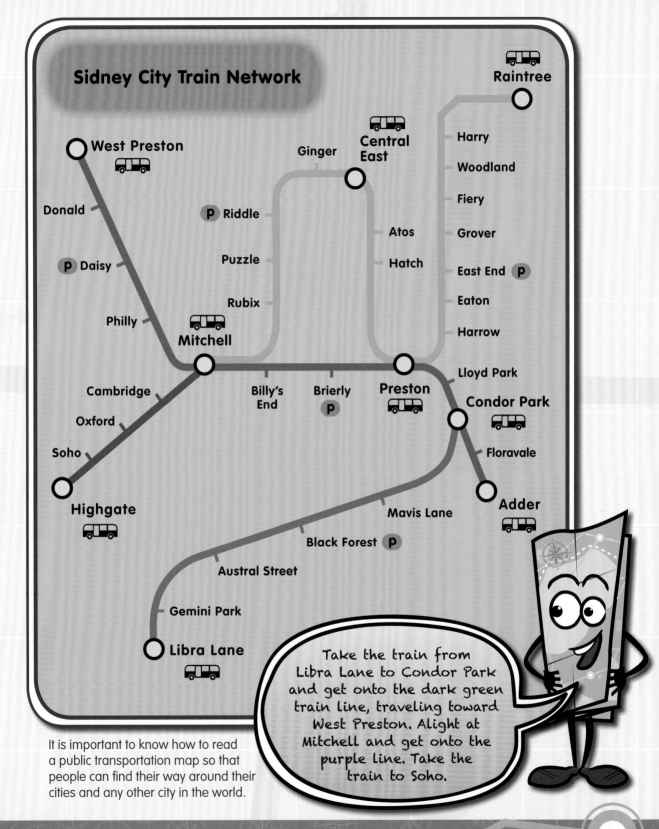

Sidney City Train Network

Raintree

West Preston

Ginger

Central East

Harry

Woodland

Fiery

Donald

p Riddle

Grover

Atos

Daisy **p**

Puzzle

Hatch

East End **p**

Eaton

Philly

Rubix

Harrow

Mitchell

Cambridge

Billy's End

Brierly **p**

Preston

Lloyd Park

Condor Park

Oxford

Soho

Floravale

Highgate

Mavis Lane

Adder

Black Forest **p**

Austral Street

Gemini Park

Libra Lane

> Take the train from Libra Lane to Condor Park and get onto the dark green train line, traveling toward West Preston. Alight at Mitchell and get onto the purple line. Take the train to Soho.

It is important to know how to read a public transportation map so that people can find their way around their cities and any other city in the world.

Reading a Building Map

Building maps help visitors to find their way around a building. Buildings that might have a map include shopping centers and malls, hospitals, schools, and museums. Buildings that are spread out over many levels have maps that may show each floor in a different color. Building maps usually have a key that explains the colors and other features. The map on page 27 uses the colors below.

- Orange represents the basement.
- Light blue represents the first floor.
- Dark blue represents the second floor.
- Green represents the third floor.
- Yellow represents the fourth floor.

How many floors up or down would you have to travel if you want to get from J & K to The Barn?

TRY THIS

The Solomon R. Guggenheim Museum in New York City has an interactive building map showing visitors where their ongoing and temporary exhibitions are located. Run your mouse over each location to find out what's there. Go to: http://www.guggenheim.org/new-york/visit/plan-your-visit/map

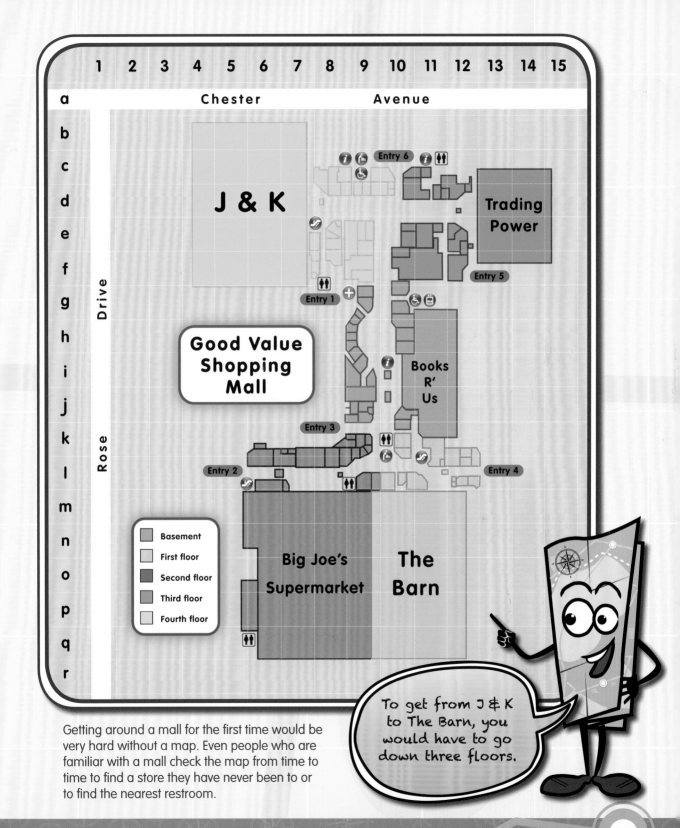

Getting around a mall for the first time would be very hard without a map. Even people who are familiar with a mall check the map from time to time to find a store they have never been to or to find the nearest restroom.

To get from J & K to The Barn, you would have to go down three floors.

ACTIVITY: Create a Community Map

Now that you know how community maps are created, it is your turn to be a cartographer. Your challenge is to draw a map of your school!

Materials You Will Need:

- pen or pencil
- notepad
- tape measure or measuring wheel
- compass
- large sheet of paper
- ruler

STEP 1

Surveying the Location

Walk around your school and take note of its features, including:

- the name or number of every room
- where the outdoor areas are
- which corridors the rooms are in
- where the exits and entrances are

Using your tape measure, record:

- the distances between all the rooms and all the other features
- the lengths of the corridors

Use your compass to figure out the direction that each side of your school faces. To do this, stand in front of the school and find out where north, south, west, and east are. Remember, your compass will always point north.

Decide On the Scale of Your Map

When you have measured the school and all of its features, measure the piece of paper that your map is going to be drawn on. Now figure out the scale. For example, if your school is 100 meters long and 50 meters wide, and your map is going to be 1 meter long and 50 centimeters wide, then your scale is 1:100. That means you have to reduce the size of everything by 100.

Prepare the Grid

Draw a grid on a large sheet of paper. The grid should be made up of vertical and horizontal lines, all of which are the same distance apart.

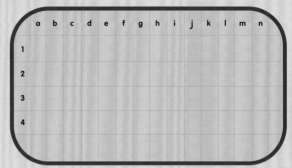

Draw Your Map

On the grid, mark the distances between the features and their directions, then draw each feature and any symbols on the map.

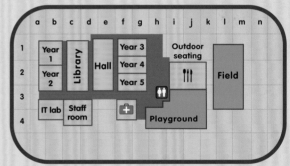

Check the Accuracy of the Map

When the map is ready, walk around the school with the map as your guide. This will help you figure out how accurate the map is.

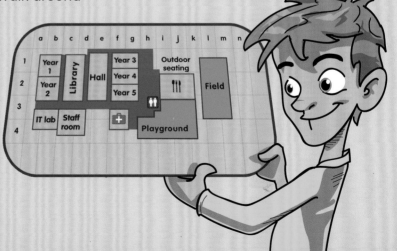

Quiz: Are You "Map Smart?"

Try this quiz and test your knowledge of community maps! All of the answers can be found in this book. Write your answers on a piece of paper and turn to page 32 to check if you are right. If you answer all 10 questions correctly, you can consider yourself "map smart!"

1 True or false? A map of a country is a community map.

2 What is the name of the compass that appears on a map?

3 Does elevation refer to length, width, or height?

4 Which of the following is a real grid reference: A1, AA, or 11?

5 When referring to a scale, what does 1:1,000 mean?

6 What type of map is a map of a zoo?

7 What is the name given to a person who creates maps?

8 What does this symbol represent on a building map?

9 What does the letter "p" represent on a public transportation map?

10 What does this symbol represent on a street map?

> Good-bye! This is where I leave you. I am sure you are now "map smart." The next time someone asks you for directions or asks you to draw a community map, you should know exactly what to do. Well done!

Glossary

accurate
correct, having no mistakes

angle
slant

campus
the grounds of a school, college or university

contour lines
lines on a map that join points of equal elevation to show high and low areas of land

elevation
height above sea level

facilities
services

horizontal
flat or level, parallel to the ground

key
a list of the symbols used on a map, explaining what they mean

precinct
an area or building that has a defined boundary

reality
real life

route
a path or way of traveling from one place to another

satellites
artificial objects sent into space that travel around Earth and usually collect information

scale
the relationship between the size of something on a map and its size in reality

surveying
measuring the features of an area of land to accurately determine the distances and angles between them

vertical
pointing straight up and down

Index

Answers to the quiz on page 30: 1. false   2. compass rose   3. height   4. A1   5. It means the map is 1,000 times smaller than the area is in reality.   6. precinct map   7. cartographer   8. elevator 9. parking lot   10. bicycle lane